CANNABIS PRODUCTION

A Step-by-Step Guide to Growing Weed at Home

BAILEY YATES

Table of Contents

CHAPTER ONE

CANNABIS PRODUCTION

A Step-by-Step Guide to Growing Weed at Home

Cannabis sativa, Cannabis indica, and Cannabis ruderalis are the three plants that make up the Cannabis genus, all of which have psychoactive properties.

One of the most widely used drugs in the world is made from dried flowers harvested from these plants. Some refer to it as marijuana, while others refer to it as weed.

The names for weed are changing as it becomes legal in more places. Increasingly, the term "cannabis" is being used to denote marijuana.

There are those who believe it's a better name. In comparison to terms like "weed" or "pot," which some people associate with the drug's illegal use, others think it's a more neutral term. Due to its racist connotations, the term "marijuana" has also fallen out of favor.

Marijuana is commonly used for its sedative and calming properties.' Chronic pain, glaucoma, and a lack of appetite are just a few of the conditions for which it is prescribed by doctors in some states in the United States.

Keep in mind that despite the fact that cannabis is derived

from a plant, it can still have both positive and negative consequences.

Cannabis has a number of different components, which we'll go over now.

Cannabinoids, the term for the diverse chemical compounds found in cannabis, number in the hundreds. In the meantime, experts don't know exactly what each cannabinoid does, but they have a good handle on tetrahydrocannabinol (THC) and cannabidiol (CBD) (THC).

Both have their advantages and disadvantages:

- CBD. Non-intoxicating and non-euphoric, this psychoactive cannabinoid does not get you "high." Inflammation and pain can be alleviated by using it. It may also help with nausea, migraines, seizures, and anxiety. " (Epidiolex is the first and only FDA-approved prescription CBD medication. Some types of epilepsy are treated with this medication.) There is still a lot of work to be done in the field of CBD's medical applications.

• THC. THCA is the primary psychoactive constituent of marijuana. THC is the cannabinoid that most people think of when they think of cannabis.

CBD and THC are the two most common cannabinoids found in cannabis products, but they can also be combined. Most people associate cannabis with dried flower, which contains both cannabinoids, but some strains have more of one than another. Hemp is high in CBD but low in THC.

Marijuana has a number of short-term effects.

Short-term effects of cannabis use can vary widely. In general, some are beneficial, while others are more problematic.

In the short term, some of the more desirable effects include

- relaxation
- giddiness
- heightened awareness of the world around you, including the sights and sounds

• a rise in hunger

perception of time and events is altered

• focus and creativity

In products with very high concentrations of CBD, these effects tend to be less pronounced than in those with low concentrations of THC.

For some people, cannabis can have negative side effects. The following are possible side effects:

- issues of coordination
- sluggish response time
- nausea
- lethargy
- anxiety

increased blood flow to the heart

reduces the heart rate

- paranoia

CHAPTER TWO

CBD-rich products, on the other hand, tend to have fewer of these side effects.

A person's consumption method has an impact on the short-term effects of cannabis. Within minutes of smoking marijuana, you'll start to feel the effects. The effects of cannabis take longer to kick in if you ingest it orally, such as in a pill or food.

In addition, there are a variety of strains of cannabis. Different cannabis products are categorized into one of these loosely defined subcategories. Here's a brief overview of some of the most common strains and their possible effects.

Marijuana's long-term effects have yet to be studied.

The long-term effects of cannabis use are still a mystery to researchers. Some of the existing studies have only looked at animals, and there is a lot of conflicting information out there about this issue.

To fully understand the long-term effects of cannabis use, a number of large, long-term studies in humans are needed.

Development of the brain

A study published in 2014 suggests that cannabis may have a negative impact on adolescent brain development.

Those who begin using cannabis in their teens are more likely to suffer from memory and learning issues than those who do not begin using cannabis in their teens, according to this research. However, it's not clear if these effects will last.

People who begin using marijuana in their teens are more likely to develop mental health issues later in life, such as schizophrenia, according to a study published in the journal Pediatrics. Experts, on the other hand, aren't quite sure how strong this connection is.

Dependence

Cannabis can also lead to dependence in some people. Some people report feeling irritability, a lack of appetite, and mood swings when they stop using cannabis.

People who begin using cannabis before the age of 18 are four to seven times more likely than those who begin later in life to develop a cannabis use disorder, according to the National Institute on Drug Abuse.

Problems with the lungs

Cannabis smoking has the same health risks as smoking tobacco.. Perhaps the airways are irritated and inflamed.

Tobacco has been linked to bronchitis, and it may also increase the risk of COPD (COPD). Studies have shown that cannabis use does not cause lung cancer. This is an area that needs more study.

Is the use of marijuana legal in the United States?

Despite the fact that it is still illegal in many places, the use of cannabis for recreational and medical purposes is gradually becoming more widespread. Recreational and medical marijuana use are now legal in several states across the United States.

Medical marijuana is legal in some states, but not in others. Cannabis, on the other hand, is still illegal in the United States under federal law. Inflammation and pain may be alleviated by using CBD. In the treatment of some types of epilepsy, Epidiolex has been proven effective.

Laws regarding cannabis vary from country to country. Cannabis use is illegal in some jurisdictions, while others allow the use of products containing only CBD.

It's important to check the laws in your area if you're interested in trying out cannabis.

Needed materials:

Seeds

Soil

Containers with drainage holes for growing plants

Increase the amount of light (wattage information below)

a compact floor fan

Vitamins and minerals (fertilizer)

A light-proof grow area, such as a tent.

Scissors

A bottle of misting spray.

The first step is to germinate the seed.

That last bag you got from your boy had a seed in it, and you were fortunate enough to find it. What are my options at this point? You want to germinate your seed to ensure that it is viable before you plant it. First, put some damp paper towels in an airtight container and put the seed inside; close the container and place it somewhere that isn't too hot—think of the top of your cable box or refrigerator as an example.

If the seed is viable, you'll see a tiny white tail poking out within one to three days. You need to find a new seed if you don't see a tail in five days.

Try germinating multiple seeds at the same time. Until your plant begins to flower, you have no idea if you have a male or a female. Your chances of getting a female plant go up when you have more than one of them in your collection. Male plants, on the other hand, produce only pollen, not flowers, which is what you're looking for. Small hairs called "nodes" appear at the base of the stems of female plants

CHAPTER THREE

Second, sow the seeds.

Choose a container with holes for drainage and a standard potting soil mix. A plastic Dixie cup with drainage holes drilled in the bottom is the simplest and most commonly used container. Your exposed tail should point down when you plant your seed. Clean water should be lightly misted over the top of the container before it is placed in sunlight or a grow light (using a compact fluorescent [CFL] light works well here).

You'll notice the first set of baby leaves sprouting from your soil in about two to three days. SUCCESS!! It's time to show off your accomplishments! The most difficult step has been completed!

Use a misting spray bottle to apply water to baby plants instead of pouring it directly on top during the first few weeks of their life. During the first few waterings, the seedling may "float" on the surface of the soil because it lacks a mature root system.

Step 3: Make it visible to the world

Choosing the right lighting is critical, and there are nearly infinite options available. For an indoor grower, this is often the most debated topic. With so many options available for indoor lighting, I believe that LED lights are an excellent choice for the new grower because of their low cost and versatility. LEDs can be used at any stage in the life cycle of a plant. Traditional indoor plant lighting, such as high-pressure sodium (HPS), metal halide (MH), or good ol' fluorescents, can be expensive and produce a lot of heat (FL or CFL).

Using "Blurple" colored lights is a bad idea. Although they're less expensive, the purplish color can make it difficult to see your plant's true colors and be taxing on the eyes. The true color of the leaves can be seen much better when working with lights that have a natural appearance.

Step 4: Growth of the plant

It will take some time for your new baby to reach sexual maturity and begin to bloom, so give it some time to grow before expecting those lovely flowers. The amount of space and lighting power you have to work with will have a significant impact on this step. To put it another way, 75 watts per square foot is a good general guideline.

At a minimum, you should leave your grow light on for 18 hours a day, but you can leave it on 24 hours a day if you'd like to keep your baby growing for as long as you like. If you use a standard potting soil mix, you don't need to add fertilizer or amend the soil because it already contains all the nutrients your baby needs.

Using cheap soil is a no-no, so don't do it. Investing a few extra dollars in high-quality soil will save you time and money in the long run and ensure that the plant has enough nutrients to thrive. You're looking for plants with medium-dark green leaves that don't have any brown patches.

The final step is to place the plant in a flowering pot.

The final place your baby will call home for the rest of its brief existence is here. If you're going to use a pot, make sure it holds about one gallon of soil for every foot of expected plant growth. In preparation for planting, mix one-fourth cup of granular bloom fertilizer into the soil before you begin transplanting. Often referred to as NPK, bloom fertilizers have higher concentrations of phosphorus and potassium and a lower nitrogen content than regular fertilizers (5-10-10).

Using a granular fertilizer that releases slowly throughout the life of the plant makes growing that much easier. As a result of its slow-release action, the plant is fed every time it is watered, removing that sense of uncertainty: it has all the nutrients it needs. How much or how little did I do?

When moving plants from smaller containers to larger ones, be gentle. The roots of many plants are fragile and easily damaged. Use your other hand to support the plant's root mass while gently flipping it into the cup if you're using a Dixie cup.

Forcing it to bloom is the final step.

It is necessary to "force" marijuana to flower, which is its natural cue to begin reproducing, because it is a photosensitive plant. Many people are familiar with the 12/12 cycle: a period of light and darkness lasting for 12 hours each day. An area with uninterrupted dark time should serve as the final resting place for your plant for the remainder of its life.

If you can afford it, a small closet or a grow tent can be a good place to start. It's all you need is a simple 24-hour appliance timer that can be set to run for 12 hours on and 12 hours off.

Recommendation: Choose a location for your flowering area where it will have uninterrupted access to light. Pollen sacs are formed on the female plants when the night cycle is disturbed, and these female plants are then pollinated and produce seeds when the night cycle is restored. When a plant produces seeds, the quality of your flowers will be reduced.

Relax and watch it grow.

Allow nature to take its course for the next eight to nine weeks. Only water when the top 3 or 4 inches of soil are dry, and be sure to move your grow light upward as it develops. You want to keep your light at least 12 to 24 inches away from the top of your plant to avoid the problem of "light burn," which occurs when the plant's tops overheat.

Flowers begin to form in the third week of this stage and most finish after eight or nine weeks of growth in a 12/12 light cycle. When the larger leaves begin to turn yellow and 75% of the pistols on the flowers turn red or brown, your plant is ready for harvest (also known as buds).

CHAPTER FIVE

It's a good idea to keep your grow area ventilated. Indoor gardening necessitates adequate ventilation. The addition of a small oscillating fan to your garden will help to keep it well-ventilated. As much air circulation as possible is necessary for plants to use CO2 during photosynthesis.

Step 8: It's Time to Harvest!

The day has finally arrived after weeks of anticipation and

watering. Harvest time has arrived! By the eighth or ninth week of pregnancy, your baby is ready for delivery via cesarean section.

Hang the plant upside down in a cool, dark place to dry. You can keep it in the same place you grew it if you turn off the light. You'll want to manicure the plant after allowing it to dry for seven to ten days. Remove any leaves that aren't connected to bud sites or smaller leaves that don't look "frosty" by trimming off the last of the leaves and trimming around your bud sites. At this point, you've finished!

Leaf raking is a common household chore.

If you want to get the best and smoothest smoke possible, you should simply put your flowers in an airtight container and "burp" them every day or two. By allowing the chlorophyll in the leaves and flowers to degrade, the flavor of chlorophyll is revealed and fresh buds are avoided. There are no hard and fast rules here; it all depends on the flavor profile you're going for and how long you're willing to wait for it to cure.

It's a good idea to keep an eye out for the smell of your plant when it's about to be harvested and for a few weeks prior to harvest. The use of some kind of smell control is recommended. Carbon filters, which are mesh tubes filled with activated charcoal and drawn through with an air fan, are the most common product made to alleviate this problem; the filter absorbs particulates and removes odors while cleaning the air. If you want to ensure that only the people who you want to know about your growth know about it, it's worth the small investment to do so.

THE END

www.ingramcontent.com/pod-product-compliance
Lightning Source LLC
LaVergne TN
LVHW010509160826
845677LV00012B/2758

* 9 7 9 8 8 4 7 3 3 2 6 7 5 *